RESCUE YOUR LATE PROJECT

Mark J. Woeppel

TABLE OF CONTENTS

Surveys of thousands of project managers and owners worldwide confirm our experience - that projects are rarely delivered on time or within budget. Typically, managers discover the project is going to be late in the final stages of the project. You don't see it coming until it's too late. Everything was "green" until it wasn't. All parts of the project were close to being on time. Until suddenly, they weren't. If you had known earlier, you could have made more straightforward changes that wouldn't be as costly and damaging as your choices now.

That light at the end of the tunnel? It's definitely a train. So, what to do?

Most managers assume that late projects are the result of poor planning. If we had planned better, we would have finished on time! There is some truth to that; there are good and bad planning techniques, but it's not the only component to delivering on time.

To recover the project, you must be nimble during execution. If you're not, your excellent plan will not matter. And when your project is running late, making a new plan won't help you catch up.

You must take a two-pronged approach. First, stop losing time by focusing on your project delivery processes for the work before you. After you've conquered that, you can analyze the work coming at you. In a sense, you are working to gain control of time. The top priority is getting a firm grip on the activity and risks[1] you're facing now and tomorrow, which will give you room to work on risks affecting next week and next month.

---

[1] The PMBOK® makes a distinction between issues and risks. Issues are things that have happened, risks are things that might happen. In this book, I don't make that distinction. Issues create risks that must be acted upon, so I'm using the terms synonymously.

PROJECT RECOVERY

The recovery plan has two objectives: one, to stop losing time, and two, to regain lost time. They have different teams and work on different time frames. To prevent losing time, focus on the near term (days and weeks). Work on the medium to long-term (weeks to months) to regain time.

To stop losing time, you must get a handle on short-term risks to eliminate progress-stopping surprises. Resolving short-term risk is a day-to-day activity. To recover time, you must systematically reduce medium to long-term risk; this is a daily activity, a process.

The goal for your recovery strategy is to have a reliable and credible plan and process that will deliver the project outcomes at a specific date. The "deliverables" of the recovery strategy are a well-defined project delivery system, a realistic plan, and a team that can reliably execute. A system of project management that closes the loop between the project plan and the delivery process to achieve the project objectives.

Stop Losing Time

One of the biggest challenges in a late project is to stop falling further behind; this is your first step -to stop the bleeding. Instead of re-baselining the project plan, focus on the execution process first. Preventing things from worsening has little to do with the project plan; the fact that the project is late tells you that no one's using it.

Your first objective is to get control of the work before you. 'Control' means you can reliably predict what work will be accomplished, who will do it, and when it will be complete. To achieve control, change the team dynamics and build a disciplined collaboration process.

Reset Project Expectations

Projects typically go off the rails in the later stages of the plan. Late-stage emergencies make sense, as there is often plenty of time to overcome early delays. However, the late stage also means that the team and stakeholders gained new knowledge in the earlier stages. New information often reshapes project requirements. Before proceeding with the project management tasks, ensure your team works towards the proper aims. Reset the project success factors. What does 'done' look like? How will the project be governed?

Define or redefine the mission with the project sponsor, customer, and owner. When the project is late, tensions run high, people are on the defensive, customers are angry, and team morale is low. Therefore, having a sponsor or steering committee with the appropriate level of seniority sends an unmistakable message to all stakeholders that this work is of the utmost importance.

Governance is about decision rights; who gets to make decisions? Who is accountable for what outcomes? When must decisions be escalated to higher levels of management?

Revisit the governance structure to answer these questions:

- How will we measure project delivery performance? Who will measure and report it?

- Who decides on project changes? What is the process?

- Which parts of the project or departmental functions receive help?

- When should leaders intervene?

There can be no ambiguity of authority and accountability. If your project is in trouble, review your project charter and, if necessary, rewrite it.

Regaining Control

There are six steps to regaining control of near-term risks. Your goal is to achieve the *Basic Collaboration* level of maturity using the Project Execution Maturity Model.

1. Get your team looking and working out in front of any problems.

2. One team, one goal to speed up decision-making.

3. Task priorities are stable; they do not change daily, so resources can work on each project task until they are fully complete.

4. Increase the rate of completion by systematically leveraging the project's bottleneck.

5. Quicken the execution tempo to resolve risk quickly.

Once you have accomplished these things, you can focus on future risks to regain time. That starts with how well your team manages and delivers the work before them.

Visualize the Project

The team must see what's coming to handle what's coming. Present your project visually – so your team can quickly communicate and grasp the project status. A visual representation of the project helps your team see where they are, where they're going, and the obstacles to moving the project forward. Visualizing your project or portfolio process prevents information overload while exposing previously hidden problems.

The visual project board (VPB) is not a substitute for the project plan; it's a summary outlining its decision steps or significant milestones:

- What does 'done' look like? Clearly defined deliverables.

- What is the path to 'done? Defined decision steps or stage gates.

- Who is responsible for accomplishing the work? Accountability by name.

The VPB eliminates the debate about the status of the work so the team can move into action. It provides tangible feedback that everyone can see and understand. It saves time. Team members can see the focus areas if there's a bottleneck or blockage. The problems are visible - no longer hidden. It eliminates the meetings about completed work, forcing the team effort into action and helping them to get out of the weeds and into the most critical issues that block progress.

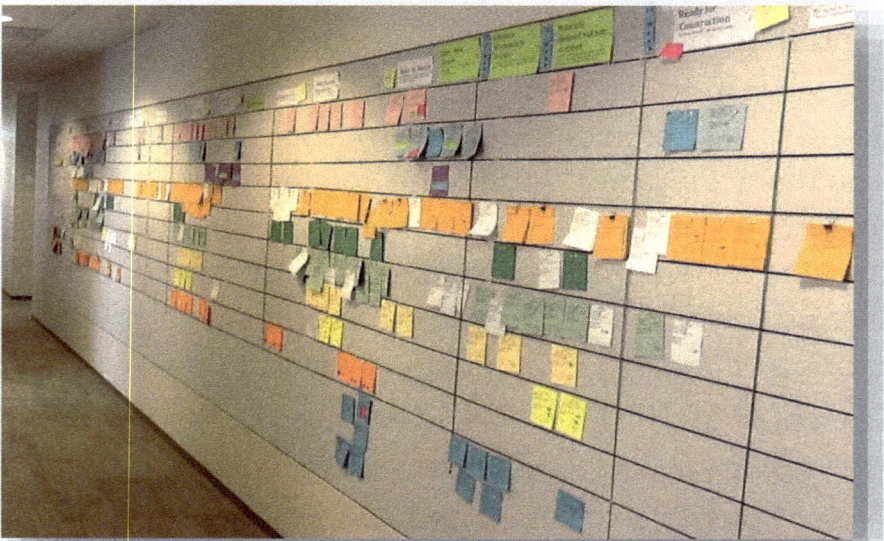

Build a Collaboration Process

A significant reason projects become late is that the team does not understand the behaviors and processes that are needed to manage the project delivery systematically.

Typically, what passes for a delivery process is merely a series of emails, status meetings, and negotiations. There is no agreement on HOW the plan will be carried out; it will just be a bunch of meetings and badgering to meet deadlines. Meetings are not a substitute for a process. What's needed is a formal practice that eliminates uncertainty and reduces schedule risk.

This collaboration process manages work within windows of time: now, near-term, later, and long-term; it defines the methods and actions to eliminate schedule risks.

First, the information that the team uses must be accurate and unambiguous. There can be no disagreement about the project's status; its progress and condition must be transparent. There can be no wasting time wondering which team member has the ball; team member's roles and accountabilities must be clear.

The VPB is your view of the field of play; each player must have their area to manage. Collaboration is not an accident; it requires leadership and structure. Like in any collaborative activity (even a game of Monopoly), you must have the rules and roles spelled out. To create a collaborative team, you must create an atmosphere of trust and accountability.

The objectives for collaboration are:

Team **productivity** – they should be working on only the most critical issues. So, your project meetings must be short, focused, and action-oriented.

Speed – The team should be answering the question, "What do we need to do *now* to make progress?"

Accountability – Direct the right people - regarding responsibility, authority, or ability to take the appropriate action.

Transparency – there should never be a question of where the project is relative to its completion and who controls that status. Transparency is the primary purpose of your VPB.

Don't make your process complicated; make it simple. Start with these rules:

- Meet face to face for 30 minutes at least once a week, standing up. Face-to-face for accountability, weekly, to set your execution tempo, and standing up to keep the meeting short. In the Kanban method, these are called stand-up meetings.

- During stand-up meetings, focus on what is _to be_ done, not what _has been_ done. History is for analysis, not collaborative execution. Push those issues and comments offline, separate from the collaboration meeting.

- Don't wait for answers from your teammates. Establish a maximum 24-hour response time for all inquiries.

- Every task has a deliverable owned by a person (not a function or department). Answer the question of who has the handoff from one task to another.

- Decide who gets to change the project and under what conditions.

- Who sets the work priorities? Ideally, the project delivery date will determine when work gets done, but there is always new work, changes, and other projects, contending with the available resources.

- What happens if team members disagree on a course of action? There must be a clear escalation and resolution process in place.

In the stand-up meetings, you will not:

- Blame someone or some organization for errors or delay

- Ask for task progress. Instead, you'll ask for the remaining time until completion.

- Analyze problems

Following these simple guidelines will transform your teams. You find that:

- People communicate regularly as part of their work process. They are not just having coffee but having purposeful discussions about the work to be accomplished.

- Teams focus on action to move the project forward, not on analyzing missed commitments.

- You will find that the team is engaged in solving problems. When problems arise, the entire team will pitch in to overcome them.

- There are no "heroes", and you don't need them to save your project.

Focus on the Future

Most people think that when a project is late, it is because the project schedule is defective - this is partially true, but it's not the main reason; all plans are inaccurate to some degree. Before you fix your plan, ensure your team can focus on the future and consistently execute *any* plan with a theory and process that delivers consistent results.

Focusing on the future has three behavioral elements:

- Identification of risks (uncertainty)
- Mitigation or elimination of those risks
- Quick Response

The objectives of this part of the collaboration process are:

- Risks do not delay the project (within limits because risk mitigation is not free)
- Risks do not increase costs
- Risks do not sacrifice project deliverables.
- The frequency of decision delay is minimized.

You can measure your team's future focus when the project is visualized and broken down into deliverables. Measuring the correct behavior builds accountability and reinforces the activities that lead to rapid project completion. Counting the frequency of the risks that never become blockages will tell you if the team focuses on the future. Calculating the duration of active risks will communicate how quickly the team responds.

On the VPB, tag blocked tasks with a red dot note and tag potential blockages with yellow dot notes.

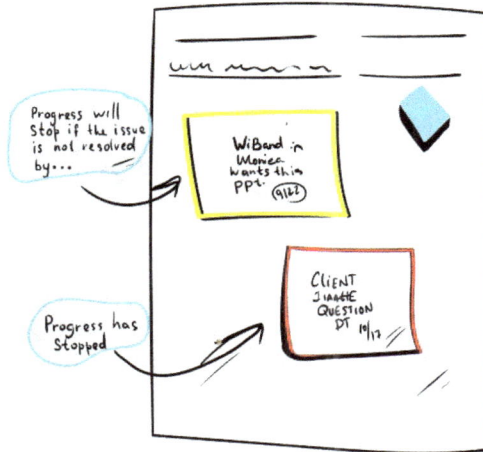

Count the yellow and red dots and convert them to a trend chart.

Proactively identifying risks is measured by the number of yellow dots per week versus the number of red dots. If people systematically identify risks, the quantity of yellow dots will rise or stabilize, and red dots will decline or stabilize. Managing your project team's ability to focus on the future is as simple as that.

Risk Mitigation
Yellow vs. Red vs. Resolved

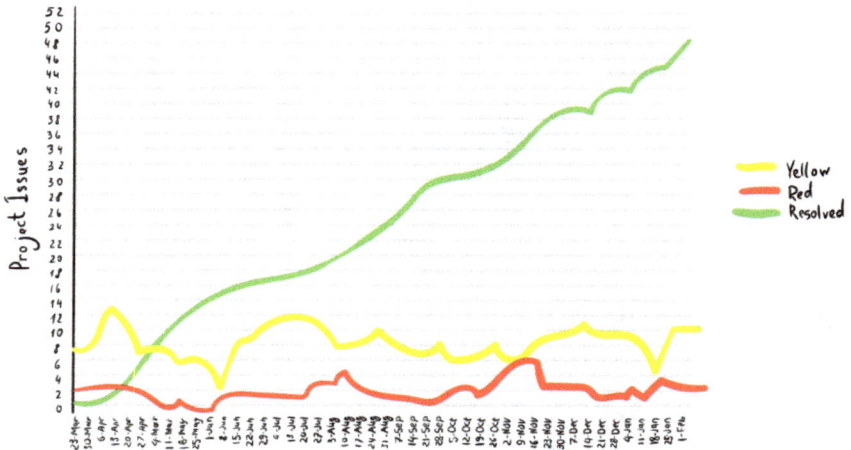

The single most significant time element in project delivery is wait time. To stop losing time, you must eliminate delays in decision-making, approvals, and resource allocation. To measure promptness, we quantify the duration of a dot. We want a quick response to any risks that may stop project progress.

REDTAG REPORT

Project Manager	Project	Process Step	Task	Issue	Date Identified	~	~	~	~	~	~	Days with resolution
~							15-Sep	23-Sep				Resolved
~							10-Sep					
~												Resolved
~							9-Sep					Resolved
~							14-Sep	22-Sep				Resolved
~							30-Sep					
~							26-Sep					

We must resolve issues rapidly →

Average Days to Resolve: 12.75

Reinforcing future-oriented behavior will transform your team's dynamic. Rather than excuses, they'll bring solutions. Rather than surprises, you'll find alternatives: fewer obstacles and faster progress. You'll stop losing time because your team is looking ahead. They're systematically solving problems before they affect the progress of the project. That's what you want!

One Team, One Goal

Another source of delay comes from the nature of complex organizations. In matrix organizations, the project manager typically lacks the authority to direct resources or make technical decisions. She can ask for resources but usually can't allocate specific individuals or suppliers to tasks. They report to someone in a different organization with the authority and accountability for resource performance. Asking leaders for help may not get the quick response that the late project requires. These people may not have the sole objective of completing the late project. Their departmental metrics could be out of line with the project's goal, i.e., the lowest cost versus the fastest delivery.

Ideally, project team members should have a common goal and the ability to reconcile their individual or functional objectives to the project's objectives. One solution to resolve this conflict is a reorganization, which may be impractical. You may be unable to reorganize and assign resources 100% of their time to the project.

Managing Performance

To avoid losing time, the team must minimize or eliminate delays in decision-making by minimizing organizational boundary friction[2]. The performance management process aims to get quick, positive responses from the departmental team members during project delivery.

A scoreboard for the project team goes a long way toward aligning the team's goals and getting the work moving forward. The scoreboard measures both the outcomes and the behaviors that create them. You can classify the needed behaviors by management level.

_____

[2] Organizational friction is the result of misalignment of goals and expectations within the organization. The less individuals and teams are aligned to consistent goals and objectives and the more they are given autonomy, the greater the opportunity for organizational friction.

Executives	Establish project priorities Resolve resource allocation conflicts Appprove or deny changes in scope, schedule or budget Direct/Lead process improvements
Project Manager	Identify projects risks Develop and launch risk mitigation efforts Exploit constraint resource(s) Resolve task priority conflicts Identify process improvement opportunities
Task Manager	Move resources to and remain until completion of the correct tasks Set work priorities for resources Exploit and subordinate to constraint resource(s) Control Work in Progress Eliminate risk as quickly as possible
Resources	Work as fast a possible on tasks Complete tasks at 100% quality Report time to completion, rather than percentage complete

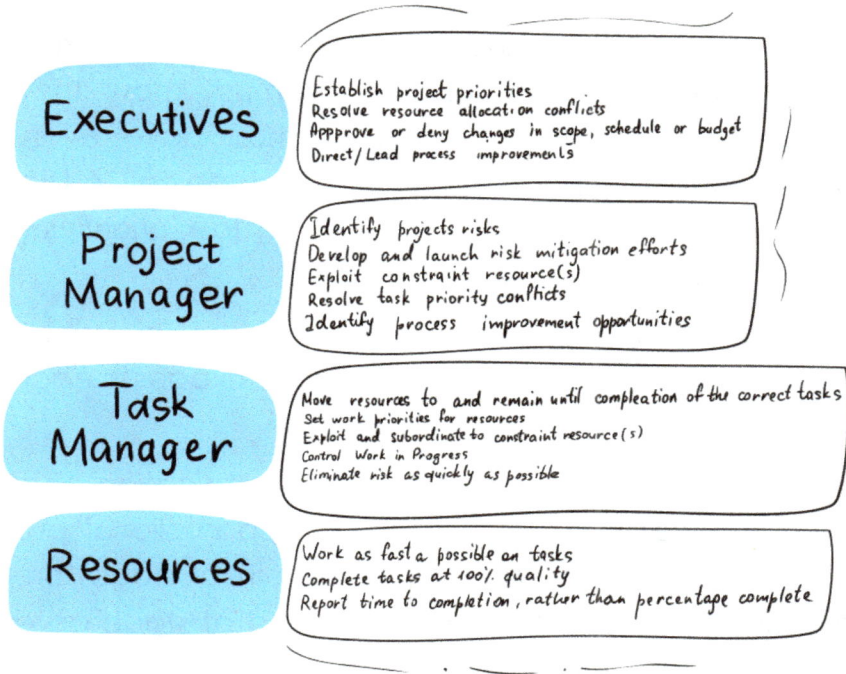

The critical behaviors to monitor are:

- Move resources to and remain until completion of the correct tasks.

- Exploit the capacity constraint resource

- Prevent overloading the delivery process with unnecessary work

- Quickly respond to risks

- Consistently break bottlenecks

- Identify and resolve risks early

- Do the work right the first time

Move resources to and remain until completion of the correct tasks. Department heads must know the most critical tasks, and the resources must have everything available to complete them without stopping. To facilitate that, they need full-kit[3] processes and task priorities (these come from the stand-up meetings).

Completion velocity is measured using the Throughput KPI, typically a count of completed work packages in each time frame.

The Throughput KPI provides an early indication of overall performance. If you're managing a portfolio of projects, analyzing trends in throughput by project stage forecasts overall throughput, typically measured at stage gates. For example, you would count the number of projects finished in the appraisal stage, the number of work packages completed in the select stage, the number of work packages finished in the define / execute stage, and the number of work packages finished with the final review

---

[3] Full Kit is a process that identifies all task inputs, like engineering drawings or specifications or components, and a policy that states all inputs must be present before work commences. When full kit is done correctly, people avoid having to do things like chasing down verifications, collecting additional documentation, seeking clarification from supervisors, or collecting more information about the customer. Likewise, a good full kit will ensure that people don't start working on incorrect information that will just create rework down the road.

stage. If you're managing a single project, measure work package completions from one phase to the next.

Exploit the capacity constraint resource to improve throughput. Identify and exploit the capacity constraint to prevent wasting the scarcest resource.

Once you have chosen the capacity constraint, count the work packages completed per week. The expectation is that the quantity trends up. If throughput is below target, refer to the other diagnostics to identify the cause of under-performance.

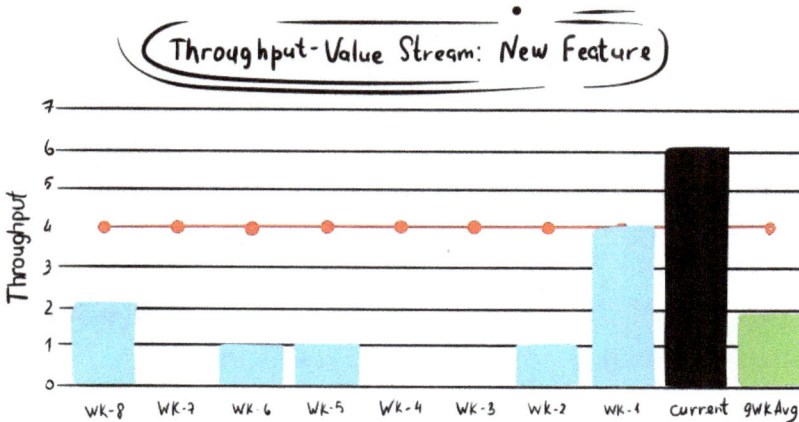

Throughput - Value Stream: New Feature

Prevent overloading the delivery process with unnecessary work by limiting the work in progress (WIP). WIP limits reduce the amount of "nearly done" tasks, forcing the team to focus on completing a smaller volume of work. Too much work in the system increases project lead times. More importantly, WIP limits improve the visibility of blockers and bottlenecks. You don't want to clog the works with tasks that do not move the project forward. To do this, you'll implement WIP limit policies (displayed on the VPB) and measure compliance.

To maximize flow (and speed) through the system, you must keep WIP within an upper and lower boundary: "WIP Target Levels".

The Diagnostic Metric WIP Target % then will measure if you are within your target range.

Consistently break bottlenecks to increase the rate of project completion. Focusing on the project bottlenecks increases completion velocity and reduces the project completion time. Multiple disciplines are required, and inter-departmental cooperation is essential.

First, we count the average days in WIP for all work packages by project phase. Days in WIP are affected by blockages in the system – where work sits longer than it should be according to your planned times. Hence, we need a diagnostic metric to track why work is often blocked so the organization can focus on the correct problems.

Then, we count the number of days projects are stuck by workstream, work element, and reason to provide an overview of the WIP – where are our problems now? It also provides a view of closed work blockages (trended) – where have our problems been?

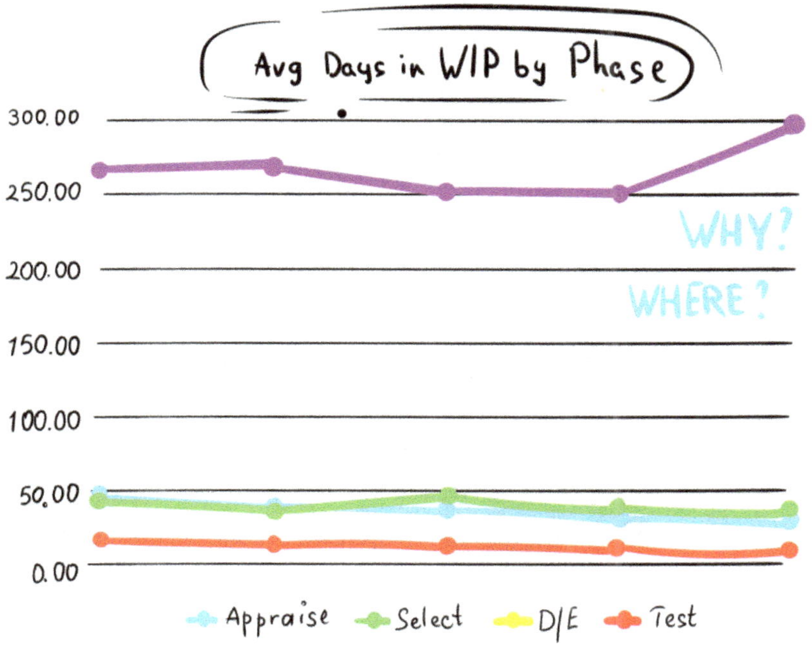
Avg Days in WIP by Phase
300.00
250.00
200.00
150.00
100.00
50.00
0.00
WHY?
WHERE?
Appraise
Select
D/E
Test

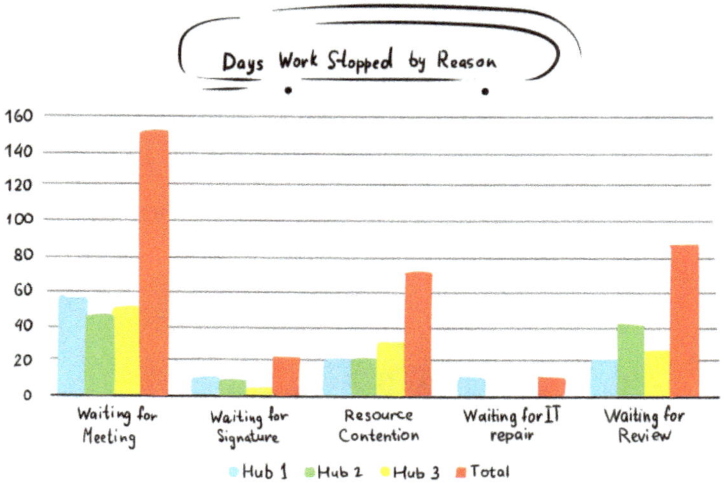
Days Work Stopped by Reason
160
140
120
100
80
60
40
20
0
Waiting for Meeting
Waiting for Signature
Resource Contention
Waiting for IT repair
Waiting for Review
Hub 1
Hub 2
Hub 3
Total

Eliminate risk as quickly as possible. When risks are identified, the functional managers eliminate them immediately to keep the project moving.

Measurement period = weekly at the weekend date

calculate days blocked open.

For each open red dot, aggregate the total days the dots have been open: days blocked open = days blocked open + (week ending date - (date red dot created))

calculate days blocked closed.

For each red dot that was closed this week: days blocked closed = days blocked closed + (date red dot closed - date red dot created)

Identify and resolve risks early to prevent work stoppages. Train the team to look ahead and find potential problems in their own and other domains.

For this, measure the number of yellow cards and those that do not go red. The idea is to encourage the team to look for risks actively and resolve them rapidly once found. Additionally, track the days to eliminate found risks and blockages.

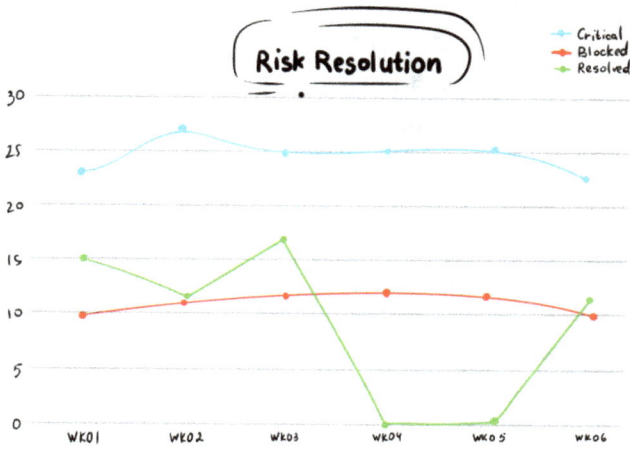

Risk Resolution

Legend: Critical, Blocked, Resolved

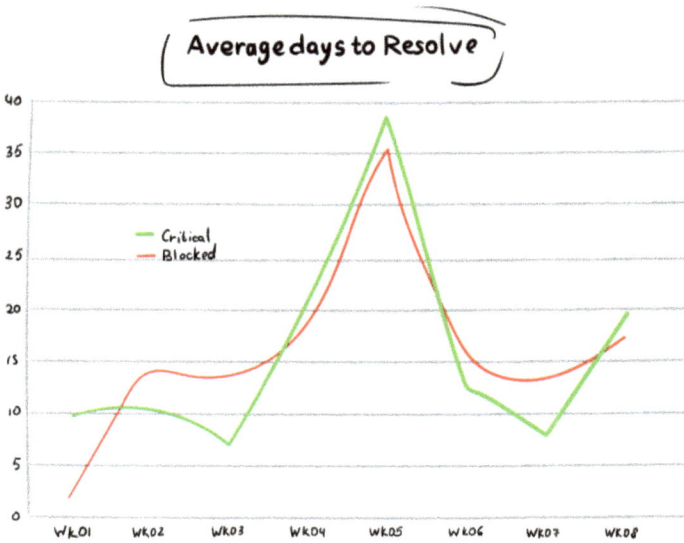

Average days to Resolve

Legend: Critical, Blocked

Do the work right the first time. Rework is always an unplanned activity that robs the project of productivity and time. Capturing that loss requires systematic management. Capture how many work packages are reworked vs. completed. The metric tells you if you're losing capacity or adding delays due to rework. Further, it provides a diagnostic function that identifies process problems.

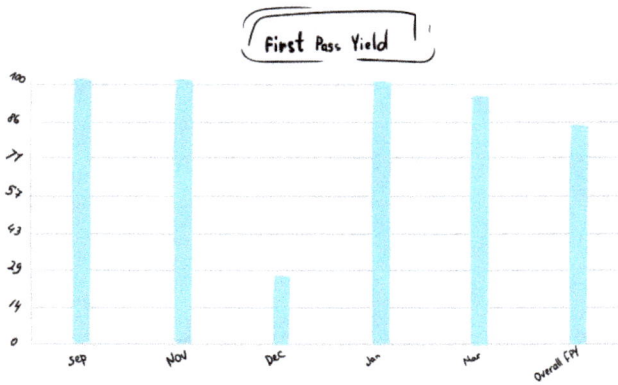

First Pass Yield

Scoreboard Summary

Behavior	Metric	What is Good
Move resources to the ready work and remain until completion.	Quantity of tasks completed per week	Increasing
Prevent overloading the delivery process with unnecessary work	WIP Target % Overall, by work element/stage	Not to exceed 100%
Quickly respond to risks		
Consistently break bottlenecks	Tasks Days in WIP	Decreasing
	Blockages by function/reason	No department or function appears as the top cause for more than 30 days
Exploit the capacity constraint resource	Quantity of work packages completed per week.	Increasing
Identify and resolve risks early	Quantity of yellow cards that don't go red	Increasing or stable
	Red cards that were never yellow	Decreasing
	Average days to resolve	Decreasing
Do the work right the first time	First pass yield	Increasing

When there is good alignment, everybody knows what their job is. They know what other people are supposed to be doing. The project gets the right resources at the right time and gets good engagement from the team members. By reducing organizational friction, productivity improves; you get the right people working on the right obstacle quickly.

Manage Priorities

Keeping a consistent priority scheme eliminates the problems created by working tasks out of sequence, reducing cascading project delays. Task switching caused by multiple priority signals is eliminated, increasing resource productivity and completion velocity, thus reducing project lead times.

Your Priority Control system maintains consistent project and task priorities throughout all projects and portfolios. It aligns local priorities with project goals and commitments that unite the efforts of the entire project team. It's transparent—everyone objectively understands how priorities are set and changed and what the most important thing to do *now is.*

The priority system need not be complicated; it must only be transparent.

To establish your priority control process, ask yourself the following questions:

1. What factors determine task priorities: the ultimate completion deadline, a significant milestone, the critical customer, or the highest-ranking supervisor? Establish a process and a final authority to remove ambiguity from priority decisions.

2. What will you use to communicate priority? Is it a date? A risk factor? The critical ratio? An objective measure normalizes task priorities across the project and portfolio.

3. Who controls them? A single point of coordination maintains synchronization among the customers and other stakeholders, even when priorities must change.

Don't ignore reality and its impact on your work priorities; recognize that surprises happen; build a mechanism to manage change without breaking the project.

Set the Criteria for Priority

- Projects with the highest priority have an arrow sticker on the project card.

- The project owner should flag the top three priority projects

- Which projects have priority for task completion,

  o Internal resources,

  o External resources

By establishing a transparent, well-governed priority management process, you'll eliminate the single most significant cause of multitasking. A robust priority control system will improve team coordination, shorten project duration, improve productivity, and reduce costs.

Closely Manage Your Bottleneck Resources

Resources are not infinite; their availability is subject to quantity and timing. Your project's performance is also determined by the team members' relationships with one another. A football team is no stronger than its weakest player. Similarly, a project is a chain whose strength is determined by its weakest link: the Constraint. In the end, the workers at the end of the process can't do any better than those at the beginning; the worst performer dictates overall project performance.

Resources are not infinite; their availability is subject to quantity and timing. Your project is like a chain, where its weakest link determines its performance. Finding and improving that weak link is critical to boosting velocity and progress. Generally, there is only one. However, when you improve that one, another will appear. These bottlenecks help you focus on the few things that will make the most significant difference in productivity and completion velocity.

If you don't effectively manage your bottlenecks, they'll manage *you*. Your teams will be chasing the latest obstacles and reacting to problems rather than preventing them. Sometimes, those obstacles may be too significant to surmount. You will simply run out of time to effectively eliminate them before they affect your project.

Typically, identifying the bottleneck is relatively easy—the weakest link in the chain is the one that has the most work piled up in front of it (it has *much* more work than available capacity) and, therefore, is the one creating the most schedule risk. It's not necessarily the slowest process, but the one with the most workload relative to its available capacity, and thus the longest queue of waiting work. So, if you want to improve the completion rate, you must find a way to increase the productivity of that link. For example, four lanes are open at the supermarket, each with ten people in the queue. When more lanes are opened, the queues will be shorter; everyone will move faster.

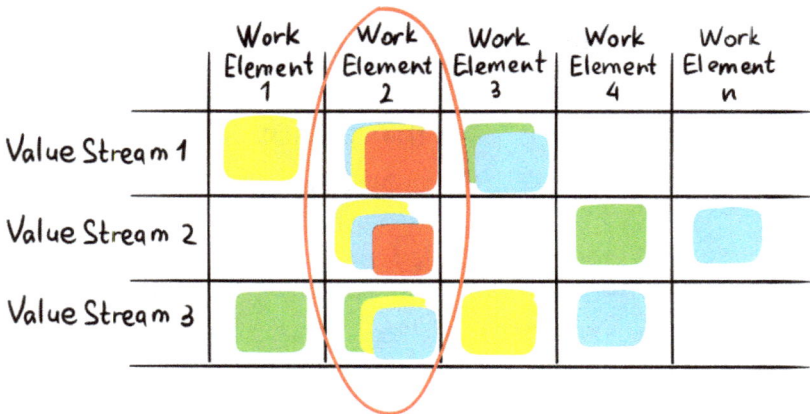

	Work Element 1	Work Element 2	Work Element 3	Work Element 4	Work Element n
Value Stream 1	🟨	🟥	🟦		
Value Stream 2		🟥		🟩	🟦
Value Stream 3	🟩	🟦	🟨	🟦	

The bottleneck will appear as a backlog of work in a process step, visible to everyone.

To manage your bottlenecks effectively, ask the following:

- Why is there so much work waiting at this step? It may not be a shortage of resources; maybe work is being released early.

- Who's going to resolve it?

By consistently identifying and breaking bottlenecks, your project will continue to roll along, maybe even accelerate. If you've visualized our project well, you'll be able to see where the bottlenecks are. You'll reduce your project duration and schedule risk. At the same time, you'll see a boost in your delivery reliability and productivity.

These strategies may not be sufficient to bring your project in on time, but it will not get later. You'll have control of the project, which will be completed earlier than when you started the rescue effort. If your project is in trouble and you have no idea what to do, these strategies will point you in the right direction. You'll be able to be more proactive, seeing and preventing stoppages. You'll be able to see the path forward to deliver on time, and your team will be moving in that direction. You need a second recovery strategy if you still think you'll be late.

Second Objective: Regain Time

Once you have control of the work before you, you can begin to work on influencing the future. Challenge everything in the plan, the deliverables, the risks, the schedule – no policy or decision is sacred. Your goal is to claw back as much time as possible, so tear down what has come before and start the project anew, systematically identifying and eliminating schedule risk.

Recovery Process Overview

1. Start with the end in mind and clarify the project charter

2. Update the work breakdown structure to align with the present situation and charter revision(s)

3. Get the work and resources allocated by recalibrating the project schedule

4. Revisit and rebuild your risk register.

5. Eliminated schedule uncertainty with a robust risk management process

Assign a person 100% dedicated to running this process – someone who can work across functions and up and down the chain of command. Your analyst must be knowledgeable about your project management software and ERP system. Lastly, you'll need buy-in and cooperation from the local process owners. The tempo of this process is weekly.

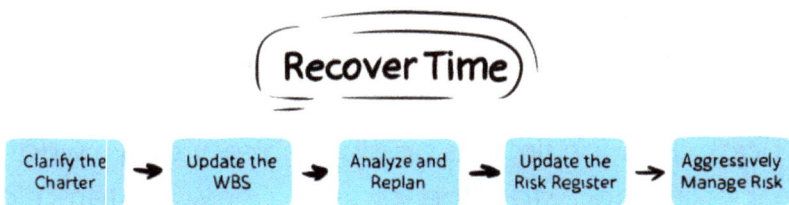

Recover Time

| Clarify the Charter | → | Update the WBS | → | Analyze and Replan | → | Update the Risk Register | → | Aggressively Manage Risk |

Test and Recalibrate the Project Plan

At this stage, you do not have the luxury of taking your time to do a full assessment, develop a recovery plan, and re-baseline the schedule. Sponsors, clients, customers, and other stakeholders will demand immediate results and corrective actions. There will be amplified management attention on the project from this point forward, so you must conduct testing and recalibration as rapidly but as thoroughly as possible. The following approach is a game plan to provide a structure that delivers results for the recovery project manager and their team.

1. Test the Project Plan – Assessment

2. Produce an Achievable Plan

3. Work the Plan

The Assessment has three objectives:

- Defining an accurate status of the project and its schedule

- Identifying the significant risks and opportunities for the project

- Establishing an extended team for the recovery effort

What is the Status of the Project?

Often, a troubled project is drowning in meetings, task details, component shortages, hot lists, and a general feeling of 'things are out of control'. You must quickly sort through these to arrive at some confidence in understanding the state of the project, so start with the visual project board and collaboration process; it clarifies the status, puts the team on the same footing, and points everyone in the same direction. And you won't be chasing your tail; the collaboration process makes room for recapturing lost time. Go over the basics of project planning.

Clarify the Charter, Stakeholders, and Deliverables

Begin with the end in mind. As the project progresses, expectations change (scope creep), and understanding of the work is clarified, not to mention that the budget has changed. Check alignment of purpose. Confirm the project outcomes – milestones, deliverables, functions, and dates with the sponsors and clients. In many cases, deliverables in the plan are out of sequence or have undergone significant changes. In large EPCI or ETO-type projects with many internal and external (customer and supplier) technical interfaces and design review processes, some goals may align with your company processes, objectives, and behaviors, and others may be misaligned. The governance on these needs to be well defined and documented to avoid delays or lack of clarity in roles and responsibilities, contractual/commercial matters, or technical authority to make decisions. For example, 3rd parties may have lump sum contracts or time/material, creating different behaviors.

Ensure you have the right stakeholders with clear accountability for the deliverables. At the very least, you'll define the customer who receives the benefit of the project, the project owner responsible for delivering that benefit, the project manager responsible for managing the project work, and the resource owners accountable for doing the project work.

Working with the customer and the project owner, restate the definition of 'done'. What physical deliverables and capabilities will be evident when the project milestones are delivered? Don't forget the acceptance criteria as well. Who says the milestone is complete, and how will it be measured?

Clarify and Correct the Work Breakdown Structure (WBS)

The WBS is the foundation of the project plan and its recovery. Look for agreement with the charter and the project deliverables – either too much or insufficient content. Explore the following:

- Does the WBS lend itself to acceptable project control?

- Does the WBS' level of decomposition reflect the level of management? Is it too detailed or not detailed enough? Are there varying levels of detail? Ideally, the WBS is tailored to the managerial level of people managing the work, which could result in multiple work breakdown structures for different levels of control.

- Is each work package described as a physical deliverable or capability?

- Are the critical milestones (like pay points) and stage gates clearly defined?

- Does the WBS include all deliverables and capabilities to complete the project?

Analyze the Plan

The analysis has two parts: fixing the dates and vetting the schedule.

Align the Dates

If you use an ERP system tied to your project planning software, there is a substantial risk of working out of sequence. Resources and suppliers may complete some tasks too early and others too late. With early completions, the earned value metric may not match the completion schedule, bloating work in progress and creating confusion in work priorities. The project can be behind schedule even though the spending shows the project to be on track. Late finishing tasks drag the project behind, forcing shifting priorities and multitasking, wasting resource capacity.

During project delivery, the customer requirements must be transparent; in complex projects, they can get obscured. Sales order delivery dates that drive ERP systems often differ from the customer's needs. These dates are important because they drive work orders and purchase priorities deep into the supply chain. Offsets in the ERP system drive purchase and production order delivery dates. In turn, resource allocations are based on these dates. Incorrect dates will cause work to be done too early, forcing spending out of sync with the project needs and diverting resource capacity from the tasks that propel the project forward. This mis-synchronization will give the impression that the project is exceeding the budget and has the potential to clamp down spending on the things where spending will make a difference. In any event, it's a distortion that prevents managers from understanding the project's actual status, preventing effective decision-making.

Some believe adjusting the dates in the system to earlier than the date the customer needs them will somehow cause the project to be delivered early. In truth, the actual dates become known, and the team ignores the formal priorities, undermining confidence in the schedule and promoting side processes to get the work done on time. In short, no one believes in the priorities, and the project team must resort to meetings and hot lists to hash out the most pressing work. Take advantage of the formal system to manage priorities.

Ensure that the formal planning system dates match the customers' needs. If you need buffers, make them explicit. Question the offsets in the bill of material to ensure they are not too conservative and are applied consistently throughout the product structure.

Vet the Schedule

Scrutinizing the schedule will shine a spotlight on future risks – those that may lie beyond the reach of your collaboration process. Pay attention to the deliverables and milestones in the WBS to ensure they agree, then examine the structure of the project plan. Test the Integrity of the project schedule using your ERP and project management software. Common planning mistakes are:

- Varying levels of detail – mixing of high-level and low-level tasks. Tailor the tasks to the levels described in the WBS.

- Missing work – things that were overlooked during the initial plan.

- Unnecessary work – things you thought you had to do, but for whatever reason, you no longer need.

- Incorrect resource allocations or overloads (dates!).

- Inflated or understated task duration estimates.

- Incorrect task linkages/dependencies (i.e., finish to finish, start to finish, etc.) – Ensure the finish-to-start linkages align with technical requirements, not preferences.

- Orphans - tasks that are not linked to a deliverable or successor.

A word here on planning granularity: your project plan at this point should be high level, based on the organizational level of team members executing the schedule. Sponsors, clients, and resource managers seek tasks and deliverables aligned with their management authority. Each resource manager may have a more detailed plan for their area of accountability, but that doesn't go in the first iteration of the schedule. Let the deliverables in the WBS be your guide.

If you're using conventional software like Microsoft or Primavera, Identify the critical path and reconcile resource availability (including subcontractors) with the planned dates. The preferred method is the Critical Chain planning system using software like Exepron. The task of re-planning will help you reimagine your project schedule and align it with your collaboration process to close the loop between planning and execution.

Update the Risk Register

The delay in your project is a clear indicator that there's room for improvement in managing uncertainty and risk. Fortunately, the PMBOK provides a robust risk assessment and management framework, and I trust you're well-versed in its principles. What's imperative now is to mobilize your team swiftly, spearhead a comprehensive update of your risk register, and refine your contingency plans. Eliminating future risks is the path to recapturing lost time and steering your project back on track.

Manage Risks

"Risk Management is how adults manage projects." - Tim Lister.

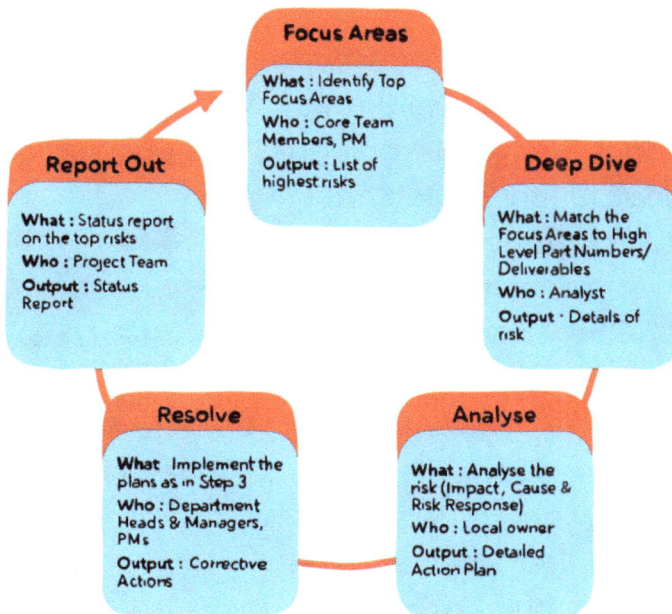

The Collaboration process helps you see the risks and obstacles that are affecting the work before you; testing the schedule will help you see future risks, those that are beyond your collaboration process and those that are not on the risk register.

This process is separate from the red and yellow dots generated in the collaboration process. The primary outcome of the collaboration process is revealing the uncertainty (risks) and obstacles presently affecting your project. The risk management process is a weekly cadence integrated with your collaboration process to head off and eliminate future risk – i.e., promised delivery dates of suppliers, production schedules, story status, or any area where a knowledge gap could affect your schedule.

Find the Focus Areas

In your collaboration process, you will undoubtedly find blockages and risks. These are your top priorities, but if you only work on these, you'll never gain time on your schedule.

You must look further out into the future. The focus areas could be suppliers, engineering, quality assurance, anywhere in the delivery process. The top focus areas will be driven by evaluating each link in the completion process - supplier delivery schedules, engineering

Focus Areas

What : Identify Top Focus Areas

Who : Core Team Members, PM

Output : List of highest risks

change notices, purchasing, production, construction, etc. If you're building complex structures, you will let the bill of material and build plan guide you to the top parts to focus on and resolve in a week. In product or software development, you'll let your understanding of features and capabilities guide you.

Deep Dive

Once you've identified the focus areas, conduct a deep analysis to get to the specifics of risk – what it is and who is responsible so you can formulate an action plan. The specifics are:

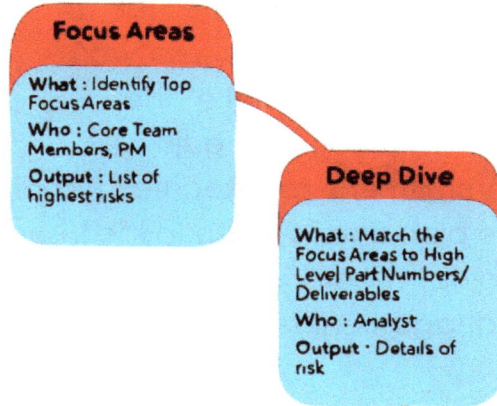

Focus Areas

What : Identify Top Focus Areas
Who : Core Team Members, PM
Output : List of highest risks

Deep Dive

What : Match the Focus Areas to High Level Part Numbers/ Deliverables
Who : Analyst
Output · Details of risk

- Engineering design processes, which could involve end users or suppliers

- Part Numbers

- Suppliers

- Contractors

- Department heads / Accountable persons

Analyze - Prepare a Response

The analysis stage further evaluates the severity and likelihood of risk impact. Prepare an action plan to address and reduce the identified risk and create alternatives to eliminate it. The department manager where the risk is found owns this plan, so work with them to make the response plan and gain commitment to execute. Report the plan and its status to the Visual Project Board and the project management team.

Deep Dive

What : Match the Focus Areas to High Level Part Numbers/ Deliverables

Who : Analyst

Output · Details of risk

Analyse

What : Analyse the risk (Impact, Cause & Risk Response)

Who : Local owner

Output : Detailed Action Plan

Resolve – Act

Implement the plan created in the prior step and follow through.

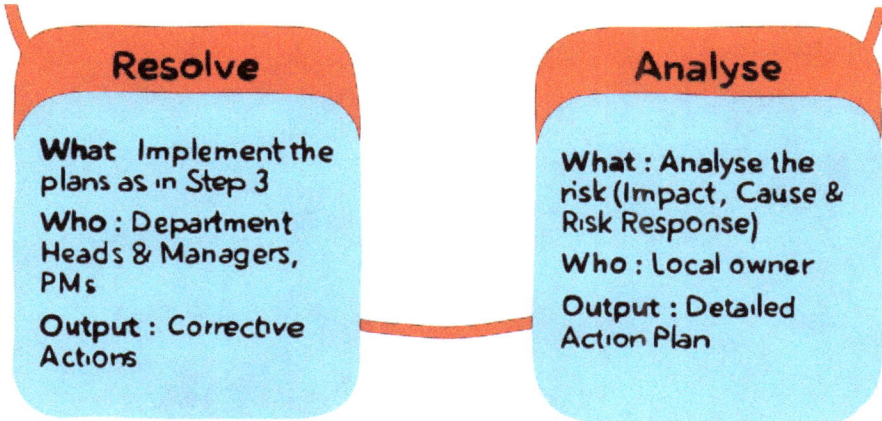

Resolve

What Implement the plans as in Step 3

Who : Department Heads & Managers, PMs

Output : Corrective Actions

Analyse

What : Analyse the risk (Impact, Cause & Risk Response)

Who : Local owner

Output : Detailed Action Plan

Report Out - Be Accountable

Be sure to report the resolution plan's results to the project team. Even if the plan was unsuccessful, there should be no ambiguity about the risk status and any next steps.

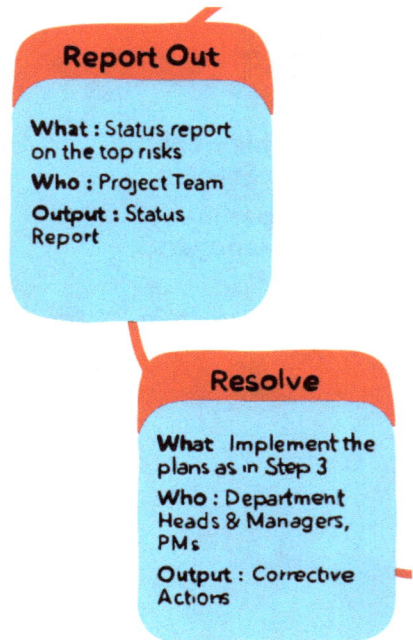

Report Out

What : Status report on the top risks

Who : Project Team

Output : Status Report

Resolve

What Implement the plans as in Step 3

Who : Department Heads & Managers, PMs

Output : Corrective Actions

Integrate the Risk Management Process with the Collaboration Process

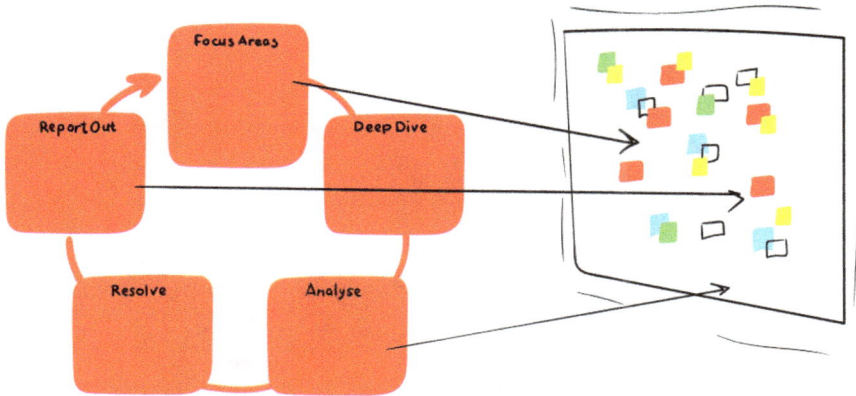

TAKE ACTION

I've outlined a two-step process, but ideally, you'll do both methods in parallel with two teams. One team focuses on stopping the loss of time, and another on regaining time.

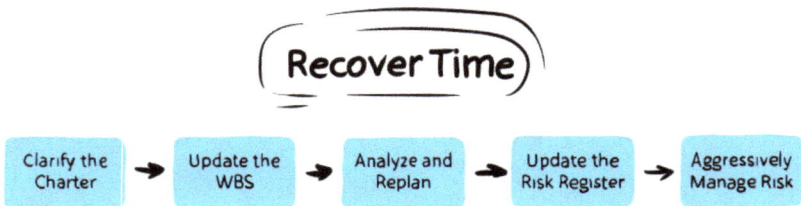

Stop Losing Time

- Visualize the project
- Focus on the future
- One team One goal
- Manage Priorities
- Manage the bottleneck

Recover Time

Clarify the Charter → Update the WBS → Analyze and Replan → Update the Risk Register → Aggressively Manage Risk

RESULTS OF RECOVERY

The process outlined here has been tested and proven many times. Every time, it delivers a reduction in completion time, an increase in speed of completion, and a dramatic increase in productivity. These results reinforce confidence in the approach and the plan.

"…it [the process] fostered better collaboration and visibility within the project team."

Project Manager

"The Project team [has] more visibility and helped make the PPMs accountable."

Portfolio Manager

"The opportunity for us is in the tens of millions of dollars a year in additional throughput and efficiency."

Group Manager

"It is by far the best thing I've encountered in my seven years here in terms of being able to track not only individual parts within a project but also those at the macro scale."

Chief Counsel

"When teams from different disciplines come in and see the same thing on the Visual Portfolio Board, you understand immediately what needs to be done. This is a big, big advantage."

Vice President and Project Manager

SUMMARY

When faced with a project in crisis, the key is decisive action. I've equipped you with two powerful tools for action: systematic collaboration and rigorous risk management. While these approaches may not guarantee an immediate turnaround, they will unquestionably prevent further delays – you'll be rescuing your project. In moments of uncertainty, these strategies serve as a clear guide, steering you in the right direction. By embracing these methods, you'll elevate your strategic thinking, chart a course to on-time delivery, and set your team on a decisive trajectory toward success.

BIBLIOGRAPHY

Ward, H. L. (2007). *Five critical first steps in recovering troubled projects.* Paper presented at PMI® Global Congress 2007—Asia Pacific, Hong Kong, People's Republic of China. Newtown Square, PA: Project Management Institute. https://www.pmi.org/learning/library/critical-steps-recovering-troubled-projects-7352

Woeppel, Mark (2017). *Simplify Your Project: How to Get the Right Work Done Without Spending Your Life In Meetings,* Pinnacle Strategies. https://projectsinlesstime.com/wp-content/uploads/2022/01/Simplify-Your-Project-new-v2.pdf

Woeppel, Mark, (2015). *Why Do Projects Succeed or Fail? The Project Execution Maturity Model.* Pinnacle Strategies.https://projectsinlesstime.com/wp-content/uploads/2021/10/WhyProjectsareSuceedorFail-PEMM.pdf

Woeppel, Mark, (2017). *ViewPoint Functional Alignment: Align Your Team with the Right Project Measures.* [Video] Vimeo. https://vimeo.com/208211982

Woeppel, Mark J., (2015). *Visual Project Management: Simplifying Project Execution to Deliver On Time and On Budget.* [2015] Pinnacle Strategies.

Becker, G. M. (2004). *A Practical Risk Management Approach.* Paper presented at PMI® Global Congress 2004—North America, Anaheim, CA. Newtown Square, PA: Project Management Institute.

Alleman, Glen, (2013). *Managing in the Presence of Uncertainty.* Herding Cats Blog, https://www.slideshare.net/galleman/managing-in-the-presence-of-uncertainty

The Manager's Resource Handbook, (2014) *Is Organizational Friction Killing Productivity?,* Blog, https://www.managersresourcehandbook.com/is-organizational-friction-killing-productivity/

Cox, Kristen, (2018), *Six Tips for Building a Full Kit,* Blog, https://www.linkedin.com/pulse/six-tips-building-full-kit-kristen-cox/

Brown, A. S. (2005). *The Charter: Selling Your Project.* Paper presented at PMI® Global Congress 2005—North America, Toronto, Ontario, Canada. Newtown Square, PA: Project Management Institute.

Sankararajan, D. & Shrivastava, N. K. (2012). *Risks vs. issues.* PM Network, 26(6), 28–29.

APPENDIX

Simplify Your Project with a VPB

The board's objective is to show the delivery process and all the work in it. It shows you *the work in the queue, the work in process, and (maybe) the work we've finished.*

Your board should fit your management scope. If you're responsible for the overall delivery process, you'll likely manage a portfolio of projects or customers. If you're leading a workgroup, it may be a skill or person.

The essential elements of the board are columns, rows, and cards. The columns are the stages of doneness.

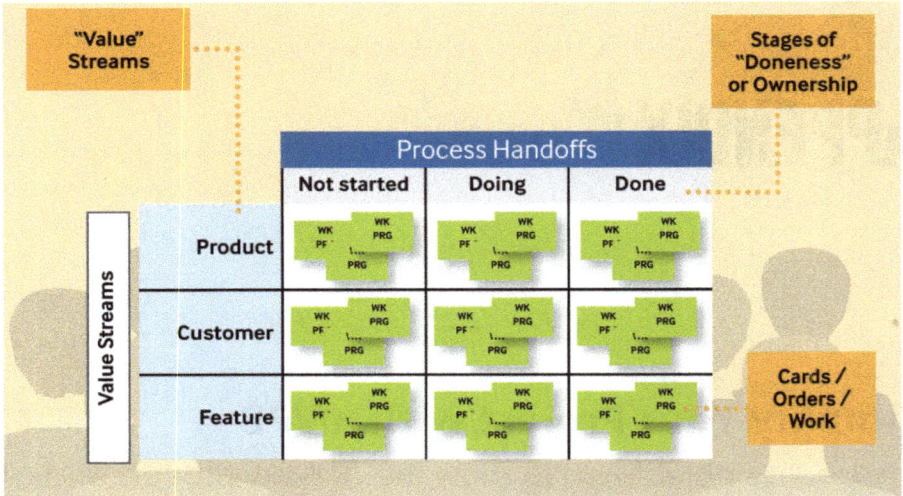

Columns represent the varying stages of doneness or ownership of the work in your project or process.

Process Handoffs		
Not Started	Doing	Done

Then, you have value categories, which form the rows. They can be products, product types, customers, managers, features, or any other way you wish to categorize the work.

Value Streams	Product			
	Customer			
	Feature			

And then you have the work, represented by cards or Post-it notes. Each card is an element of work, like a "package" that moves through your process. A work package can be work orders, features, stories, components, or whatever representation of a work unit you manage.

	Not Started	Doing	Done
Product	WK PKG / WK PKG / W PKG	WK PKG	WK PKG / WK PKG / PKG / WK PKG
Customer	WK PKG / WK PKG / W PKG	W PK / WK PKG	WK PKG / WK PKG / PKG
Feature	WK PKG / WK PKG / W PKG	WK PKG / WK PKG / PKG	WK PKG / PKG

The Process Map Guides the Design of the VPB

The first step is to create a map of your process or project. The process map defines the tasks, predecessors and successors, deliverables, and accountability under management. **Before you build a board, you must invest time in this.** This is your input to your simplification process.

There are plenty of books on process mapping, so I won't explain all the details. However, there are some critical items you need to identify. They all start with a hand-drawn map.

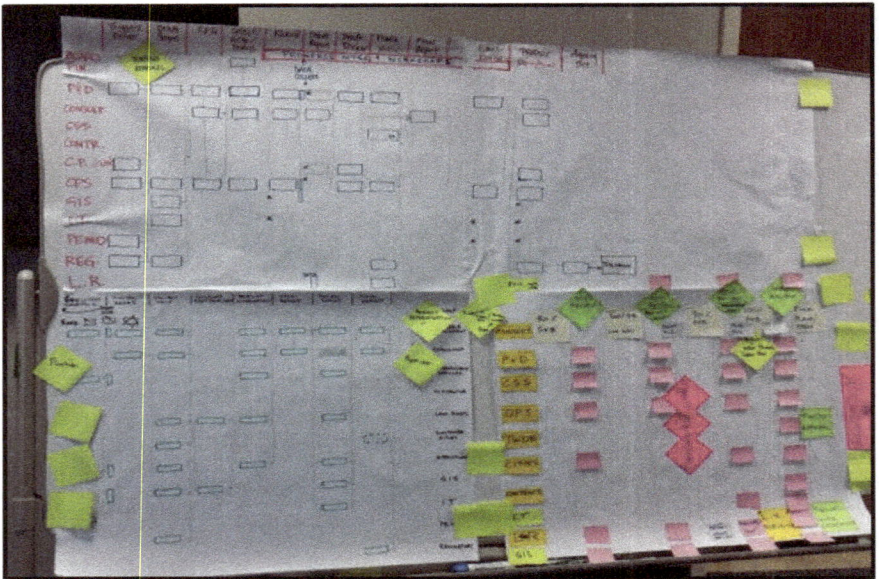

Map the changes in project or product state, transformation stages, process steps, stage gates, handovers, changes in accountability, gating processes, and decision points.

Look for similarities between projects. You're working towards distilling your project delivery process to its essence, representing your project's crucial management points.

The "management points" are critical. Identify those steps that need management or customer intervention, like approvals. These will become columns on your board.

When mapping your process, highlight:

- Changes in project or product state (i.e., groupings, design to production, etc.)
- Process steps: the technical steps your project must go through, i.e., survey, dirt work, foundation, etc.
- Handovers/changes in accountability
- Gating processes/decision points
- Similarities between projects/types

Then, take your hand-drawn version and make it easier to read. Yours might end up like the diagram below, with departments or functions in each swim lane, then progress through the columns.

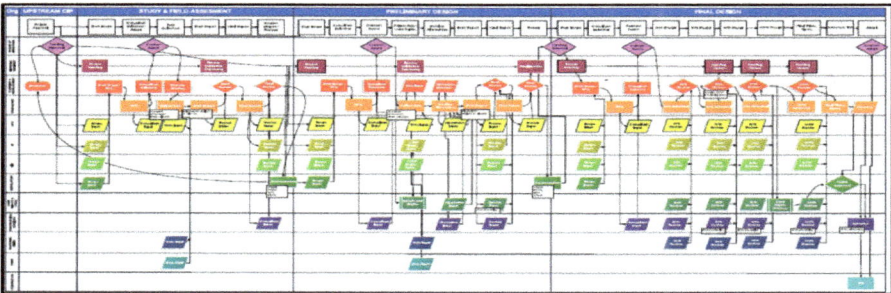

Moving from the hand-drawn to the formatted version is helpful. It gives you another chance to review the team's work in detail. Additionally, the formatted process map is a powerful tool to engage and teach your team. Often, the process map is posted near the VPB. I've witnessed several teaching moments in front of the map. An organized map will simplify communicating the details of task sequences, who does what, and when.

It's essential that you start with an imperfect VPB. Start simple, then let the board evolve into a more complex model with more columns and details. As you use it, your team will decide on the level of complexity they need.

Defining the columns

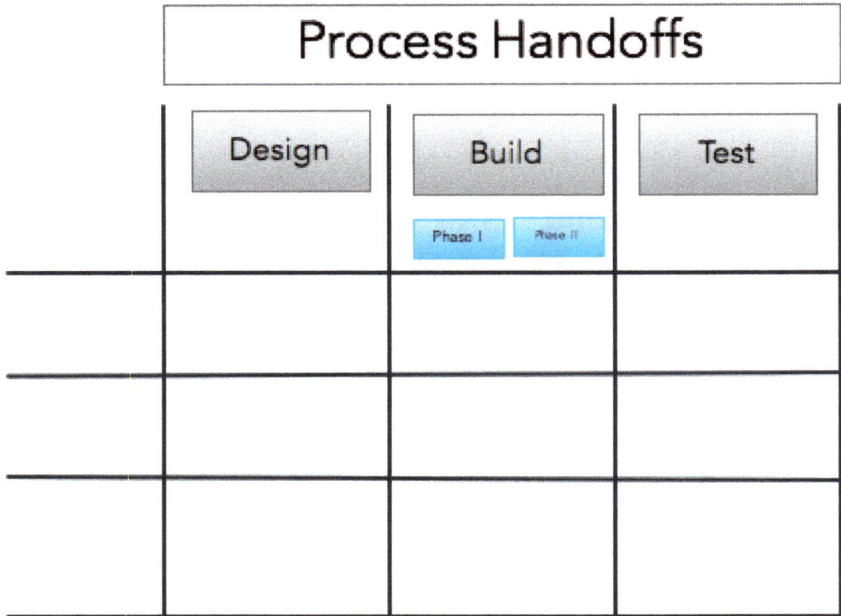

Process Handoffs		
Design	Build	Test
	Phase I Phase II	

Building the board has three steps in this order: the columns-your control points; the rows – the categories of work; and the cards – the work packages. The columns answer the question: "What are the most important processes that must be managed?" Typically, these process stages require or get the *most* attention during execution.

The columns are your management points, handoffs, project phases, and milestones. They can be something as simple as this example above.

Within each of the columns in the example above, there are sub-columns. In the example below, I have defined the major phases and two sub-phases of the project workflow.

Ready to Appraise	Appraise	Select	Define/Execute
	App | OK | Ready	App | OK | Ready	Define/Execute | Final OK

Start with headings that are descriptive summaries of what happens in that column. Don't reproduce your entire workflow or your project routing. If you must get detailed, do so around what you consider constraining or the critical processes. You can always add more columns later, but at the start, keep it simple.

Consider not just the stages but also a transition of ownership or accountability, like in different departments. Appraise is one department led by one manager. In the example below, Select is another, and Define is another. When designing your columns, you often deal with handoffs from one resource or ownership group to another.

The general rule for columns is this: if an activity produces a deliverable, it's a column. If it's a decision, it's not a column. The exception to the rule is when managing queues. You may want to maintain work queues, "ready to go". Queue columns show that the preceding work is complete. It's ready for the next stage. Another exception is when you have a bottleneck resource or a step that requires close management; this is a candidate to be a column. Follow the principle of making columns your management points.

When creating the columns, we look for similarities among projects. All projects or products will follow this same path. Consider *all* your work in the design. The board infers, "All work follows roughly the same process – the one I've defined in the columns." To clarify "roughly", some projects may follow steps that are not listed or will skip others; these should be few. If you have two kinds of workflows, you will build two boards.

Defining the Rows

The rows, called value streams, show how your product or project matures from an idea to something usable. There's an implied process ownership to each one of these value streams, although, within each column, there might be different people responsible for accomplishing the work.

The accountability categories are functional/leadership, customer, or product/project family/type. Sometimes, the category is named by location. Sometimes, it's done by resources or functions. Sometimes it's a product. Sometimes, it's work managed by a person. And sometimes, it's by the customer or feature type.

Project X					
Project Y					
Project Z					
Project XX					

Types of Rows

There are two approaches to categorizing accountability: organizational emphasis (where there is a process owner) and management emphasis.

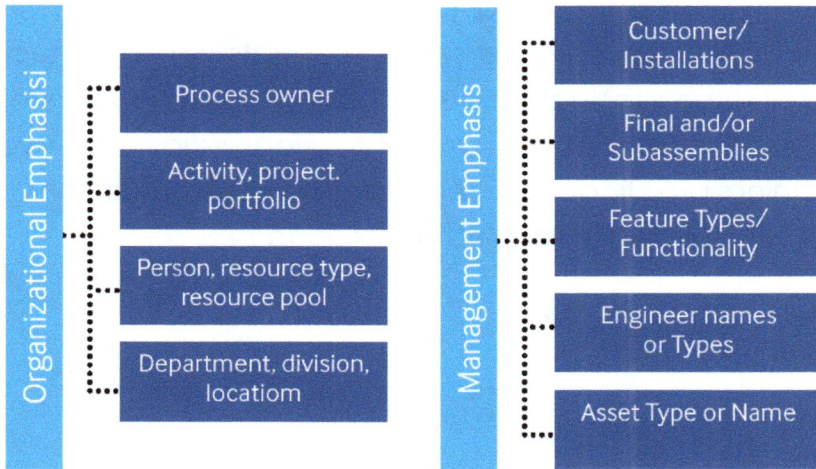

An organizational emphasis categorizes value streams around resources, activities, portfolios, or accountability. The categories could be a person, resource, resource pool, department, division, or location.

A management emphasis categorizes value streams around deliverables or physical areas. It could be a customer or installation site. It could be a work process, like final assembly or subassembly. It could represent an essential outcome, such as feature types or functionality. It could be engineering. It could be an engineer or project manager's name.

Categories of Rows

Designing your row/value stream categories starts early in understanding the workflow. The main criteria I use is the answer: Who owns the value stream or the outcome? Is it a customer or a buyer? Is it a project manager? Department head?

Not every work package or task must go through every step. We've built boards where some products will skip specific steps or some products in a swim lane will have extra steps. You should be flexible and not dogmatic. You want something practical, not a perfect representation of your workflow. You're distilling, not translating.

When you complete the rows and columns design, you can populate the board with the work – the cards.

Defining the Cards

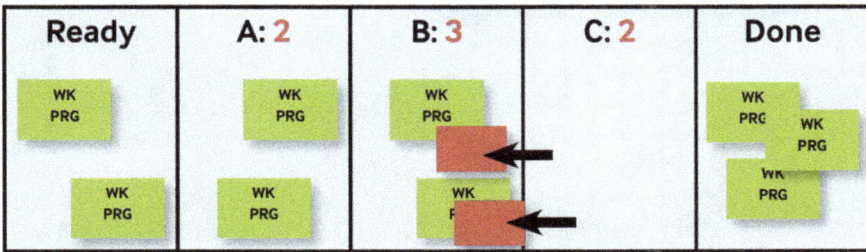

Cards, unique to your project and workflow, are representations of a unit of work - packages or work components. That unit of work can be an order, a project, part of a project, or a feature.

What is your unit of work? You may break that unit down into sub-units. For example, a work component may be pouring concrete if you're building a hotel. You could break that down to pouring concrete by floor. Sometimes, your unit of work will be both activity and time-based. The card would consist of the maximum concrete you can pour in a day. Depending on your management cadence, this time basis could be daily, weekly, or monthly.

The main principle in designing the card is to keep it simple. You may add more comprehensive information later, but initially, you want the cards to be simple and easy to maintain.

What goes on a card?

It has the project's name, the project manager's name, the amount of effort (size, type of project, lines of code, etc.), and who owns it. It doesn't have to be fancy but should be descriptive, which brings us to the size of the task.

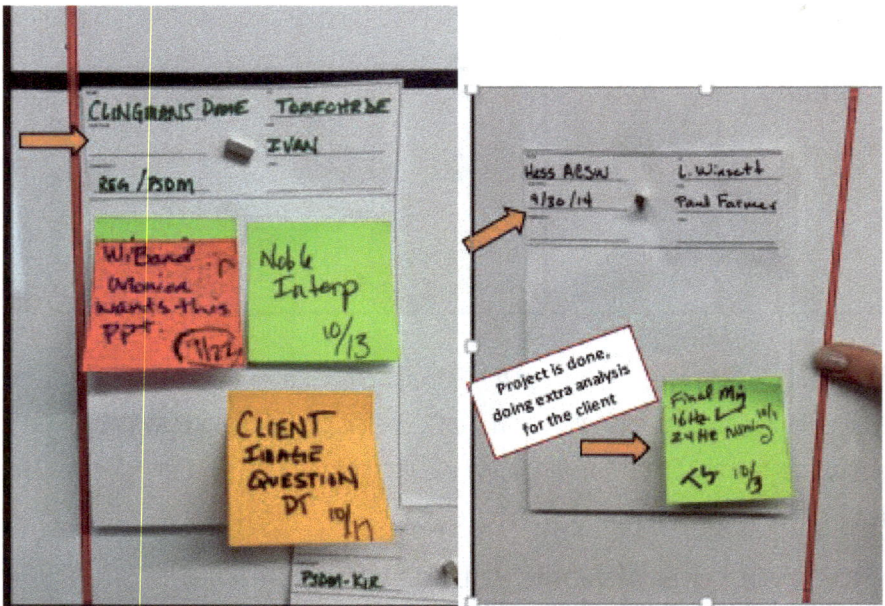

This example above has seven items on the card. It has the project name, due date, complexity, and size. In this example, the team needed some differentiation between projects. They wanted to communicate each card's approximate duration or level of effort.

Notice it says things like "Time Processing – short". It doesn't have the hours, who owns the tasks, or who does it—just the essential information.

This card doesn't have a date, but if deadlines are an important part of your process, you must have it on the card.

Another thing you can add is color. The card in the example has an orange tab on it. If you saw the board, you'd see different colors on various cards. Each color has a meaning.

Sometimes, people will put checklists or lists of activities on cards. *To complete this work, we must do these things.* Sometimes, acceptance criteria will be listed: *What does done look like?*

Resist adding more information to the cards. More information slows the time to interpret the board and increases the amount of effort to maintain it.

What follows are two cases of designing a board.

The first case is an organization that does similar projects repeatedly. They do data visualization, taking terabytes of data and creating visual representations of underground topography. The second is a one-off project.

Remember, the simplification process is:

1. Map the process or workflow

2. Decide on columns

3. Develop categories/rows

4. Design the cards

5. Populate the board with the work (the cards)

Case Study – Multiple, Similar Projects

Here is their process map.

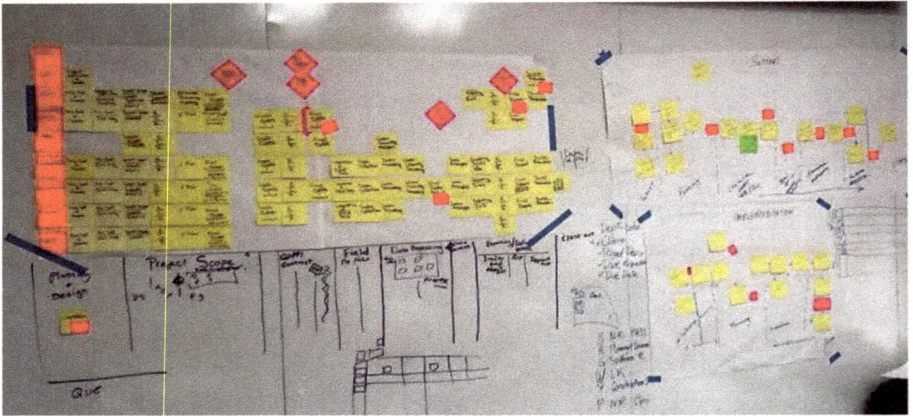

In the example above, you can see by the red Post-it notes on the left that the categories of work for this project are emerging. They named the planning, design, scoping, QA, fieldwork, and data processing steps, and they've got Post-it notes that describe the activities, as well as the task inputs and outputs.

Mark J Woeppel

Categories
- Region
- Project
- Manager

Here, they had the categories of work by geographic region. They had Asia-Pacific, Middle East, Europe, and the Americas. They had projects and managers of the three main categories of work they were managing.

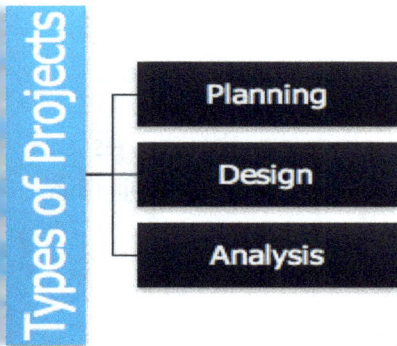

Types of Projects
- Planning
- Design
- Analysis

They also had different project types: planning, design, and analysis.

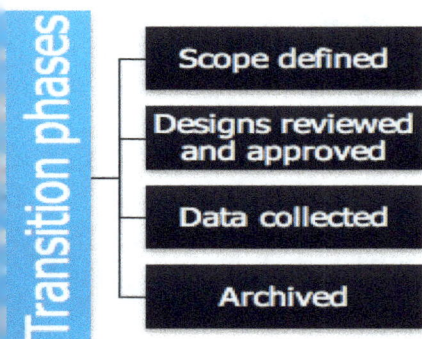

Transition phases
- Scope defined
- Designs reviewed and approved
- Data collected
- Archived

They also had transitional phases that defined the scope. Every customer and job was unique, so they had to define the project before they could do the work. After that, they had to get them approved and reviewed, collect the data, and archive it when finished.

They took this information and made it pretty.

From this effort, they defined the categories, the types of work, and the transition phases. These became the building blocks for their board. Here are the main transition phases.

And then it became a board, with just columns.

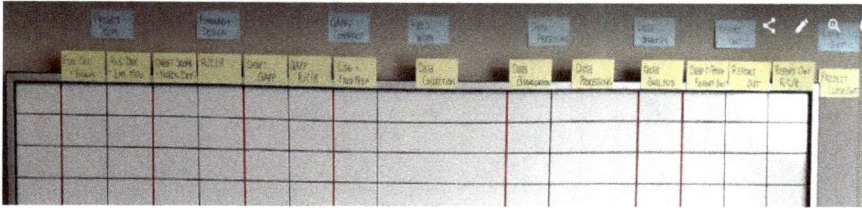

Their board maps out the high-level phases of defining the project scope, project planning and design, QA and Contract, Field Work, Data Analysis, and Close Out. These are the blue Post-it notes. They've also highlighted the decision processes with the red lines. Each decision caused a change in the state of the project, and then another decision caused another change in the state.

Then, they categorized the transitional stages, carrying over from their original hand-drawn process map. You can see those across the top of the process map and the board. These are the yellow Post-it notes, which are typically used in the early iterations of the VPB.

The first iteration of the board is derived from the process map to identify the areas to manage. You can see how they did this in planning and design, draft, scope, RCR, and project scope.

They organized the swim lanes by the project manager and then subdivided them by project.

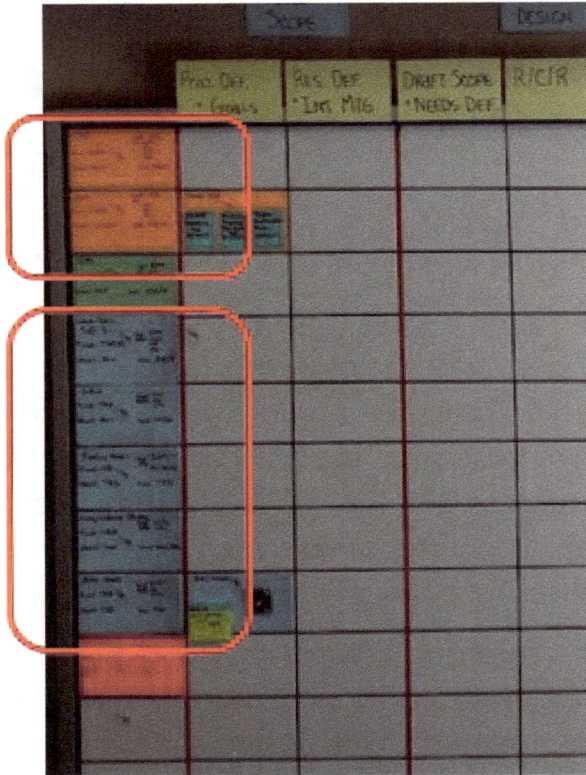

On the left-hand side, there are cards of different colors. Orange, green, blue and red. Each project manager is a different color, and each project is a different swim lane. And the projects are linked to the customer or region.

Case Study – One Project

In this case, they followed the same process but didn't have the advantage of established management points or an established workflow to use as a starting point. It's an enterprise software implementation, a project they will only do once.

This effort was about adaptation. There was a lot of configuring screens and terms, reproducing some functionality, and integrating with legacy applications. Even though there was some software development, it wasn't a full-blown product development project.

They started with a bit of raw material. The figure below is the chart they used to manage their project. There are different activities and dates across the top.

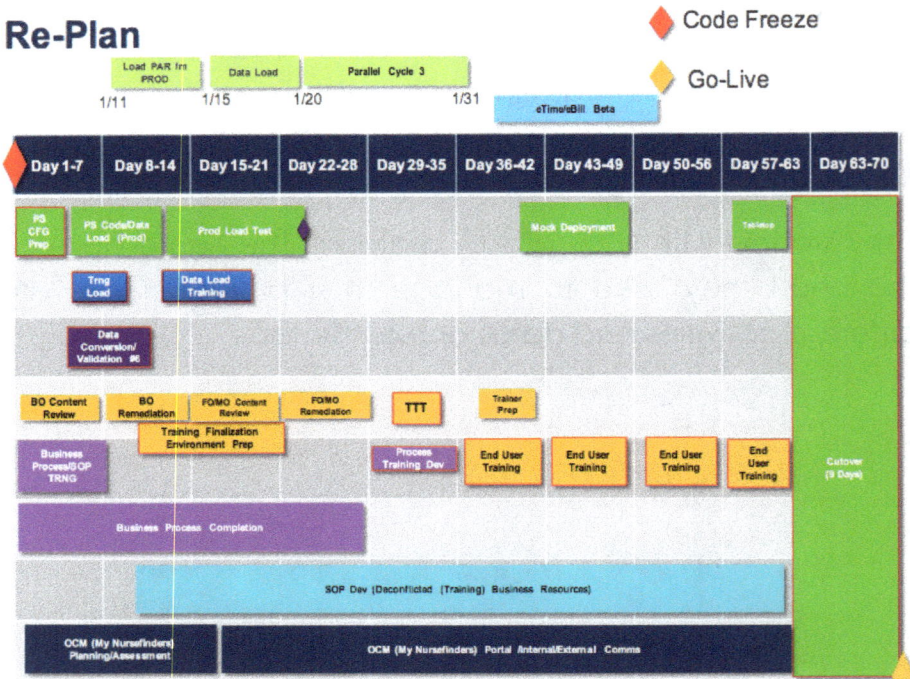

Re-Plan

The problem with this chart's method was unclear task dependencies and accountabilities. It only told them what to do. We will do data conversion, validation, back-office remediation, going to the front office, middle office content review, and then front office, middle office remediation. It has a rough sequence of what needs to be done, but the activity dependencies were poorly defined. There aren't names on it. It says, "This is the direction we need to go."

From this, they extracted some basic elements: the categories of work and work packages. It has front-office applications, back-office applications, mid-office applications, and then subcategories. They have different kinds of work, some transitional phases, and two different types of work: coding and training. This work was followed by transition phases, which were coded and then tested. We could see the conversion phases (phases 1, 2, 3, 4), which transitioned to deploy and go live. They got a rough idea of the phases they wanted to manage.

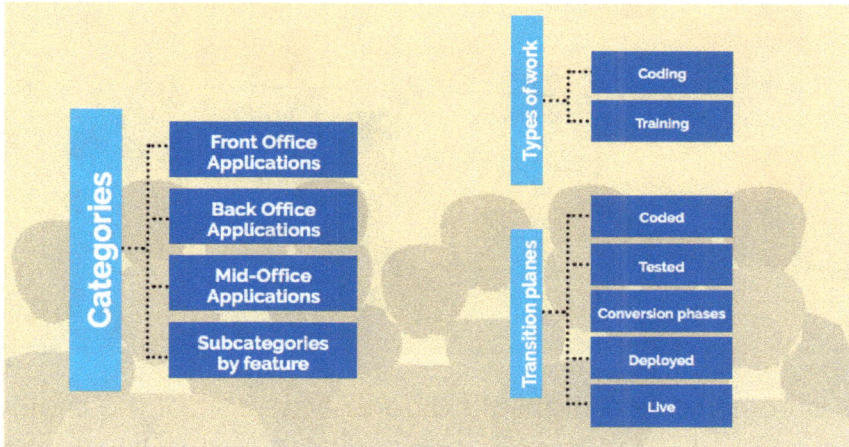

They had to make sense of status presentations, starting with a rough work categorization. They then built the connections between the different task elements and categories.

They identified the significant phases of work: code freeze, data in a training environment, load test, data conversion load, and cutover processes. They have the different resource groups for which these are needed: data group, coding group, infrastructure, and training. What was missing were the connections and the sequences.

At first, they brainstormed the tasks, the connections, and the handoffs. In our design phase, you can see all the Post-it notes.

The different colors highlight different aspects of the project. Blue represents business process activities involving the user and training communities, while red connotes IT activities.

You can also see we've drawn arrows. *This item comes before this, and it is needed for this. After they put it up on a public wall, people wrote comments like "In this, "there's partial data" or "partial load."*

This brainstorming and development were done in the open; in a hallway in one of the work areas. Putting the draft up in a public place was helpful in learning and team buy-in. Adding these comments was spontaneous (as They had hoped); sometimes, they brought people in to contribute. There were many spontaneous discussions about its meaning and accuracy in the week or so of this effort.

Working out in the open (rather than in a conference room) increased team members' engagement in the design process and the project. It helped them understand their work, what they needed to do, and the risks. Through that development, the team came to a deeper understanding of the workflow. They started seeing benefits even before they created the board.

They'd say, "*Holy cow, we've got to do this and this. Where is it?*"

And, "*Oh, here's a risk. End-to-end scenario testing – who will do that? Oh, here's another thing. They have to get those workarounds approved. What about the QA data test? Do we have or want this ability introduced into the decision-making process?*"

It's critical to get buy-in from the team whenever you're changing or working towards improvement. And if they're contributing, it's no longer *your* initiative. It's theirs. Put your draft out in the open. Let people see it. Let them contribute.

After receiving the comments and revisions, they entered the tasks and relationships into the software, organizing the presentation of the information. They then developed a network PERT diagram that showed the tasks and relationships.

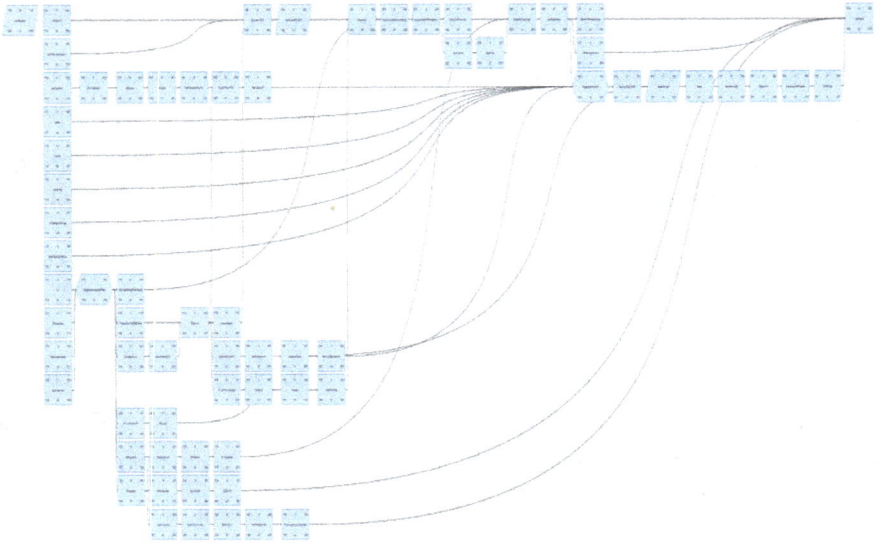

As a result, they realized that about eight things could be done immediately.

They had to figure out how to present that information visually.

Because of the analysis, they also saw different stages of the project, such as the transition from testing to release. They could take the intuition they gained in building the project networks and see where the decision points, business approvals, and functional code freezes were.

They took that network and began to develop a prototype of the board in a spreadsheet.

In the image above, notice the red blocks. These are code freezes—defined decision gates. Then, on the left are the customers affected: front office, credentialing, and back office. These became categories of work.

They started with the following process steps: the manual process analysis, the QA defects and remediation, the business approval, and the integrated stress test.

Note all these different columns in the mockup.

They designed the columns they thought were most important, put a draft on the wall, and brought the team together. They showed it to them and said, "Well, this is what we think. What do you think?"

Some said, "Oh, this is great," and others said, "Yes, but this part is not that important. We need this other thing, which is much more important than that. So, let's use that."

Then, they made another version but realized that the work, or the project transformation process, was progressing in two different ways. They couldn't create a single board with a single flow.

That forced them to separate the work into two boards: software implementation and user training.

Here's the first board. In the picture, Luis explains the board to the team. They don't have well-defined value streams; the draft workflow is on the wall.

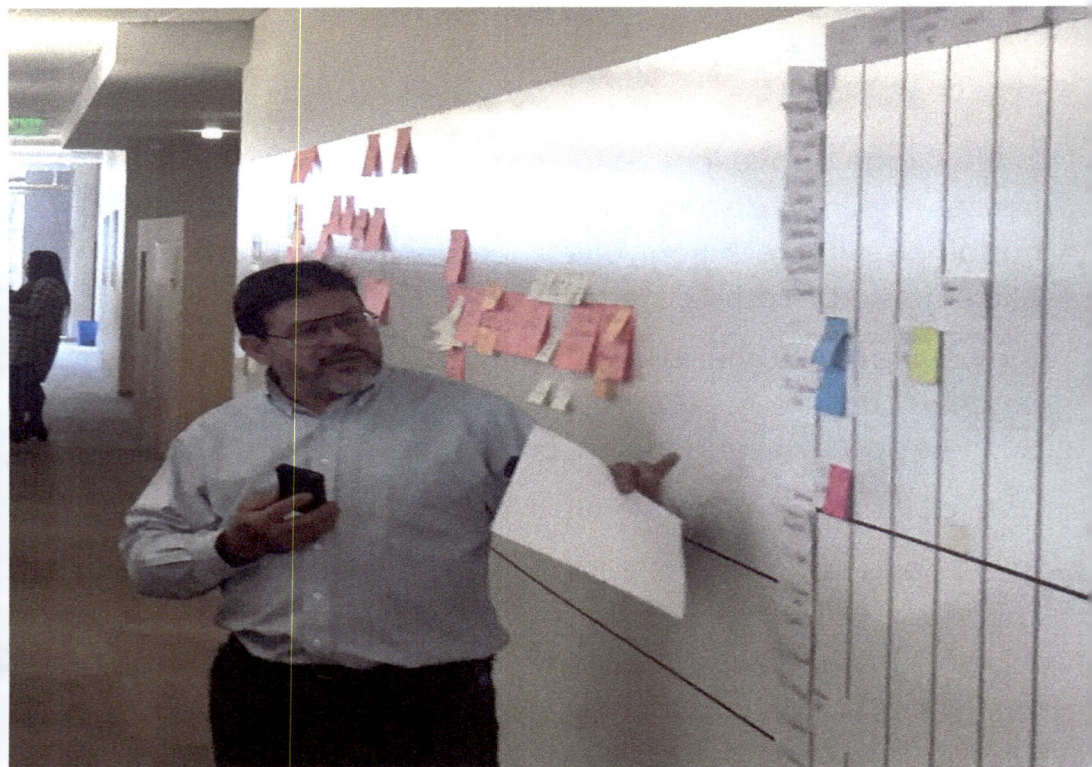

They identified the transition phases: Coded, Tested, the Conversion Phases, Deployed, and Go Live.

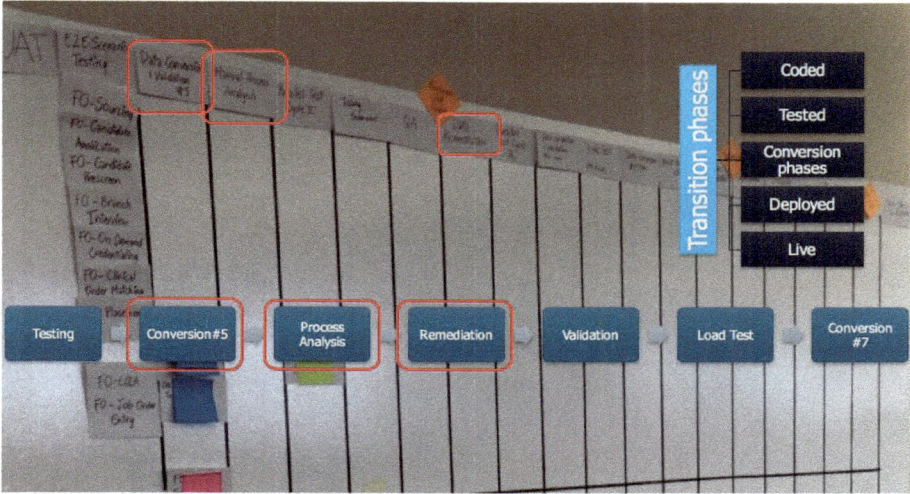

This process led to defining the columns. They went from process analysis to remediation, and the team added three more columns: parallel testing, cycle 2, the testing environment or the training environment, and then QA. The diamond up there is a functional code freeze. That's a decision, not a stage of work, but they wanted to highlight that step.

The swim lanes changed quite a bit from the first drafts. When you look at the mockup, you will see that the "front office" is a category of many applications, while the "back office" is a grouping of all the PeopleSoft applications. What they ended up with on the board was divided into front-office, mid-office, and back-office applications.

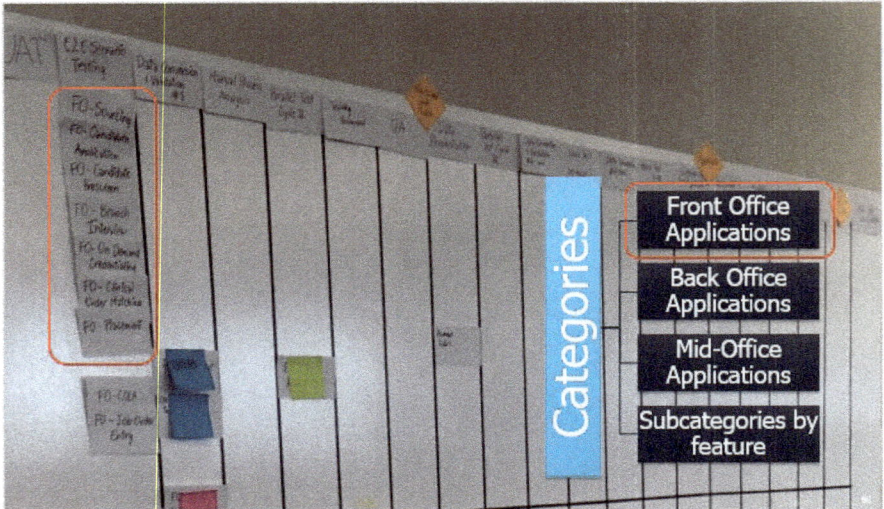

In the final version, they subdivided the front office into different features. They had front-office sourcing, front-office candidate application, candidate prescreening, branch interviews, and on-demand. Each one of these cards became a subset of front office work.

They ended up with a complex plan stripped down into features, organized by category, feature, and subcategories across the transformation process.

Lessons Learned

- Process Mapping is essential
- Start with simple representations, fight complexity
- Involve your team
- It's not about the board, it's about communication

The most important thing to do is understand how work moves from one part of the process to another, defining when a card moves from one column to another. When is it ready to move? What does "done" look like?

The process mapping exercise forces those crucial conversations and decisions, resulting in process improvements even before you get the board up, clarifying roles and accountabilities during execution.

It would be best to fight the urge (and maybe your team!) to make your board complex. People will want to add things. You must balance accepting changes to get buy-in from the team and preventing complexity.

There's no hard and fast rule about how complex or simple your board should be. It should be simple enough to use and not require too much maintenance effort but sufficiently robust to communicate the state of your delivery process and its work.

You'll know if you've struck the right balance when you can identify and assign your most important actions in less than 30 minutes.

When we start using these boards, people often fear the board will cause additional work and say things like, "Oh, my gosh... Now we've got *another* thing that we must do."

There's far less work later, which is not apparent to your team. In the beginning, your board must be simple and non-threatening. Simple makes it easy to adopt. Too much data overloads your team, and information overload is the enemy of adoption. Your board will evolve as you use it, so save time and effort by keeping it simple.

Simplifying your plan and building the board is an iterative process. Your team will not salute and follow your first version of the board. That will not happen. They will find fault with it and tell you it's wrong. Those are good things! Expect it. Welcome it. It will make your process better.

Present the board as a possibility and let the team contribute to finishing it. That way, it will become their tool. If they're going to use it, they should have a voice in building it. Typically, the board goes through four, maybe five, iterations before it settles into a final, stable version.

Once stabilized, you can use the board as a springboard for managing dates, measuring process performance, and defining resources. Don't do that at the beginning. In the beginning, focus on building a map. Don't get tangled up in detail. Start with something simple.

When you roll out your VPB, emphasize that it is not the end. The board is just the beginning. The board is a way for you to communicate and facilitate. It's the tool to get people together and accomplish what needs to be done.

Why Do Projects Fall Behind?

In the world of projects, you'll quickly find a universal truth: They have a knack for slipping through our fingers, past deadlines and budgets like elusive shadows. This tale is told across the globe in thousands of surveys—a haunting melody of missed deadlines and unmet expectations. Rest assured, for within these stories lie the secrets to redemption, the telltale signs that can serve as your compass to steer projects away from the jagged cliffs of disappointment.

Most managers blame a subpar schedule for the project's derailment. They lament, "If only we had planned better, we'd be right on track!" That's a persuasive theory. Let's see if it holds up to scrutiny.

Projects aren't neat mathematical equations that unfold predictably in spreadsheets. They're more like weather systems, capricious and elusive. Who can truly predict the weather a week down the line? Similarly, projects are riddled with uncertainty, veiled in the unknown. Uncertainty is woven into the fabric of projects – the spice makes them exciting and unpredictable. When you embark on a project, you're stepping into a world of challenges you know you'll encounter, but the full spectrum of hurdles remains a mystery. It's like navigating a maze blindfolded.

Here's a truth seasoned project managers know: Surprises are par for the course. They might be unpleasant guests, but they still show up uninvited. That's why experienced managers develop an arsenal of coping strategies: they wrangle for additional resources, camouflage contingency plans, handle stakeholders like delicate glass, and master the art of risk management. These are undoubtedly handy survival tactics, but they only scratch the surface. They're every project manager's toolkit for reacting to the unexpected.

But here's the twist: even if you're a virtuoso at project planning, your schedule will never be flawless. You can certainly improve it, but perfection is a fantasy. The real game-changer? Flexibility during execution. Your grand plan could be a masterpiece, but it's like wielding a sword with a cracked blade if you need to be more agile when it counts. If you're chasing a deadline in the rearview mirror, a fresh plan won't magically fast-forward time.

Let's agree: building the perfect plan is a lofty goal, not a realistic one. The question is, when do you sound the alarm? How do you steer your ship away from the rocks when the storm hits?

To identify the reasons for this wide range and shortage of high performers, consider what stakeholders believe are the core drivers of project success. [4]

Executives who commission projects believe detailed planning, leadership skills, and stakeholder engagement are critical. Meanwhile, project managers believe improved planning, enhanced maturity, better executive sponsorship, well-defined goals, and minimal scope changes are crucial.

Figure 1. Successful Project Completions

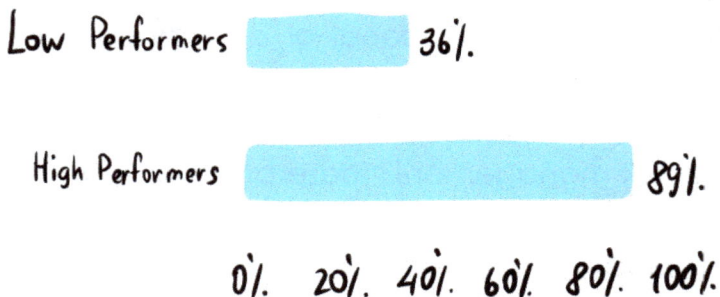

Low Performers 36%.

High Performers 89%.

0%. 20%. 40%. 60%. 80%. 100%.

---

[4] PriceWaterhouseCoopers. (2012). Insights and Trends: Current Portfolio, Programme, and Project Management Practices.

Every executive and project manager agrees that effective project delivery is critical for a high-performing organization. However, there is a wide range of success in project performance (see Figure 1), with low-performing organizations performing nearly 12 times worse than high-performing. Further, there are relatively few high performers overall.[5] Late projects are commonplace.

Living in the Past

In many projects, reporting progress is a substitute for moving forward. You must understand where you are relative to where you're going, but reporting completions is not a substitute for managing.

If your team lives in the past, they'll spend considerable time reporting "progress", including the percent completed and why jobs are late. They're a little stuck, working to understand where they are in the project. The project team is focused on sorting out which tasks are complete and negotiating which jobs have the highest priority. They're not looking *forward,* and project progress reflects it.

You won't get to your destination looking through the rearview mirror.

Working on the Project Part Time

Often, the project manager is the only person *on* the project. She is the only one accountable for the project's

---

[5] Accenture. (2014). Developing Strategies for the Effective Delivery of Capital Projects.

outcomes. She then spends her time on enrollment and buy-in activities rather than the core task of moving the project ahead. This happens so frequently that a section of the project management body of knowledge is devoted to stakeholder management.

When project team members have conflicting goals, they need the project manager's help to engage with the project's work fully; they may even make decisions that make completing it more difficult. You see this often with centralized functions like purchasing. Your project needs and priorities are only one factor in their activity. They don't respond to questions quickly, don't come to meetings, and are not working in sync with the rest of the team to move the project forward. Your project is one of many job priorities, not the highest one.

To win, everyone on the team must have the same goal.

Frequently Changing Task Priorities

The project team members have difficulty determining which tasks should have the highest priority. Job priorities shift from day to day, week to week. There is no central authority to set priorities, and resources will respond to the latest communication from a customer, friend, or boss. They'll constantly switch jobs – changing priorities for the resources (people) doing the project's work.

Priority shifting breeds multitasking, the number one killer of productivity. When priorities change, it adds more work to the project. That additional time is never in the schedule, so the project loses time, and resource productivity declines. Inevitably, the project finishes late.

Wandering Bottlenecks.

The project always needs more resources to complete the work at hand. Finding more resources is a constant battle. There's never enough time or budget. The right resources are not available when you need them. The team may feel like they're playing project "Whack-A-Mole".

Bottleneck resources limit the rate of project completion. If the bottleneck moves from one resource to another week to week or daily, it indicates a poor grasp of the resource requirements to complete the project.

The bottleneck is where you get leverage to go faster. If you don't recognize it, you're just spinning your wheels.

Slow Response to Problems

Many projects have the "I sent an email but have not gotten a response." kind of problems. Yes, the different time zones are an issue. Yes, we get hundreds of emails daily, but a delayed response to a critical problem slows the entire project down.

A slow response to problems indicates a team that needs to be more engaged. The team doesn't understand the time-critical issues, who owns them, and what is required to resolve them.

The most significant component of project duration is waiting time. The more you wait, the longer the project takes – wait time is not built into the schedule.

Diagnose Your Project. Will You Be Late?

1 pt	2 pts	3 pts	4 pts	5 pts	Score
Multiple hot lists, local preferences set task priorities, or calls from downstream customers	A formal priority control system exists but is used inconsistently	A transparent priority system is used to manage task/activity priorities	The priority control system has been in place for some time and effectively manages work priorities.	The priority system and its components are continuously refined	
Many members of the team have their own agenda. There's plenty of blame to go around!	Team members sometimes put their functional objectives over the project's objectives.	The entire project team is clear on the project objectives and KPIs.	Project team members are using KPIs to identify project process problems and improve performance	Project Team members are using KPIs in continuous improvement efforts	
Team members rarely work together to solve problems or accelerate the project.	Team members sometimes work together to solve problems or accelerate the project.	Team members routinely work together to solve problems or accelerate the project.	The project team follows a formalized process that governs how projects are executed.	The project team follows a formalized process that governs how all projects in the portfolio are executed.	
The constraining operation, process step, or resource is unknown	There is awareness of the constraining operation or process step, but we do not manage it effectively	We know the constraining operation or process step and strategies are in place to increase its productivity	Utilization at the Constraint is tracked and reviewed regularly with an ongoing corrective action process	We place the Constraint in the system where it best suits us.	

3-6 Oh yes. You will be late.

6-11 You will probably be late, but you might be able to pull it off at the last minute.

12-16 You have a good chance of finishing on time, but there are hidden risks.

17-20 Why are you reading this article? You're in great shape.

Experienced project managers and executives may still point to the plan or the assumptions behind the project plan. I have never worked on a recovery project where the project plan was acceptable or was even being used to drive the project. When turning around a troubled project, you're looking for the most significant impactful actions you can take NOW to get things moving - *leverage*. In a recovery situation, you must focus on the most critical elements that will get your project back on track as quickly as possible. You can't fix everything wrong; you must select the things that will give you the most significant results as fast as possible. Re-planning your project is an excuse to delay taking the necessary medicine to get things moving.

www.ingramcontent.com/pod-product-compliance
Lightning Source LLC
Chambersburg PA
CBHW071503210326
41597CB00018B/2668